MOUTH

MOUTH
Copyright © 2025 BECCA RAE ROSE

All rights reserved. No part of this publication may be reproduced or transmitted in any form or by any means without the prior written permission of the publisher, except for brief excerpts for the purpose of criticism and review.

For permissions and information on ordering books, contact operations@smallharborpublishing.com.

Cover art design: Beth Carlson, "Mouth"
Interior design: Brianna Chapman
Editor: Joshua Davis
Publisher: Allison Blevins
Director: Kristiane Weeks-Rogers
Managing Editor: Bianca Dagostino

MOUTH
BECCA RAE ROSE
ISBN 978-1-957248-56-1
Harbor Editions,
an imprint of Small Harbor Publishing

MOUTH

Becca Rae Rose

Harbor Editions
Small Harbor Publishing

Contents

Quadrant 1 — Quadrant 2

false — milk

incisors
canines
premolars

MAXILLARY ARCH

molars

RIGHT — LEFT

molars

MANDIBULAR ARCH

premolars
canine
incisors

Quadrant 4 — Quadrant 3

For all my pulled teeth

QUADRANT 4

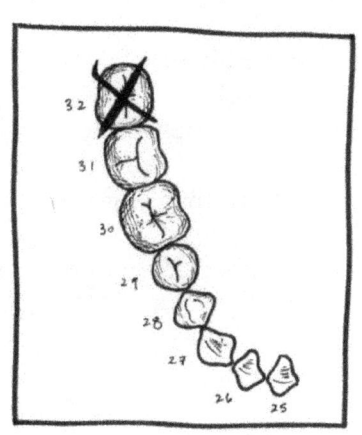

OBJECT (31)

Baby, he says, *less teeth*.

He only calls me baby because he doesn't know my name. I could be anyone. My hair, poolwet, wrapped around his fist like a snake or a rope, or something more original: leash, reins, lasso, bike chain, electrical cord, creeping vine, telephone wire. The salamander has muscles in their tail made for internal severance. It's called autotomy. To jettison their own body. If human hair had this ability, I could cast myself off with little fuss, the cells already dead anyway.

Even so, I probably wouldn't leave. Aren't I grateful to be desired? He could have had anyone. Every girl ordering another rum and coke from his bar, taking the ice cubes into their mouths one by one as he watched. My knees are held to the tile floor by more than just the pressure of his hand on my shoulder. I open my mouth wider.

TOOL (26)

You are born with every tooth you'll ever have, already waiting in the gums for their moment of emergence. There are two sets—a temporary and a permanent—and all of them were present in the womb with you, seeds in the pink-wet.

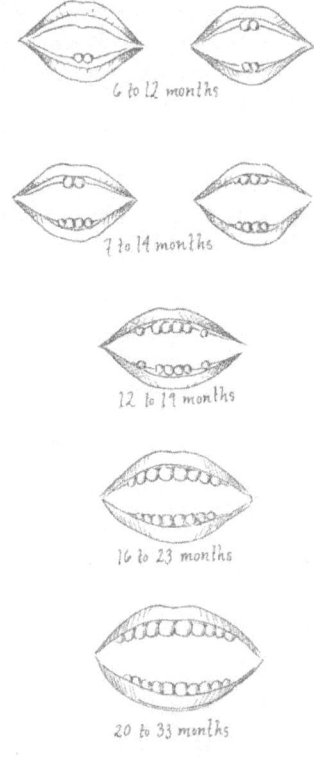

6 to 12 months

7 to 14 months

12 to 19 months

16 to 23 months

20 to 33 months

This is a defining factor of our taxonomic class, almost as much a vital link among mammals as warm blood. The bear cub, the wolf pup, the house kitten, the coyote whelp, the calf, the kid, the foal, the fawn, the fox kit—all of us, in our youth, will spit out our teeth and start again.

For the human, it takes six months as an air-breathing thing for the first set of teeth to be fully formed and ready to surface, a process called *eruption*—like tectonic plates shifting beneath the gums. The temporary set answers to many names: *baby, milk, deciduous*. All at once, they are magma, child, liquid, leaf. They arrive in a careful orchestration that takes over two years to complete: incisors, then premolars, then canines. It is a sequence of losses and gains—fluctuating configurations of form and emptiness, until the mouth, finally, is full of tools. Each has a specialized function, intended to shear, grind, or tear.

Barring accidents, the milk teeth remain until around the age of five, when, one by one, the permanent set comes in. It is a slow overtaking—it will be seven years or more before each temporary tooth has been tucked beneath a pillow or saved in a scrapbook. In that time, we grow to fit our new mouths; adult teeth are larger and more numerous to fill the expanding palate and widening jaw, and each has thicker enamel and a longer root. This is the mammal body's contingency plan: if we live long enough, we are awarded better tools to fend for, to fend off.

As our tools improve, so too does our ability to chew. By age twelve, a girl has lost all her milk teeth; she is ready for what is hardest to ingest.

OBJECT (30)

To be a successful killer, one must have sharp teeth:

    wolf;

    lion;

    bear;

    orca;

    tiger;

    cougar;

    hyena;

    cobra;

    crocodile;

    shark.

WEAPON (27)

Sharks have infinite teeth. This is not hyperbole—never in a shark's life do they stop knitting new fangs, conjuring up enamel from somewhere inside the gums, indefinitely. Like magic—or perhaps extreme resource conservation—teeth are the closest thing to bone in the shark's body, the hardest substance reserved for the mouth. Sharks belong to a class called Chondrichthyes: fish made of cartilage.

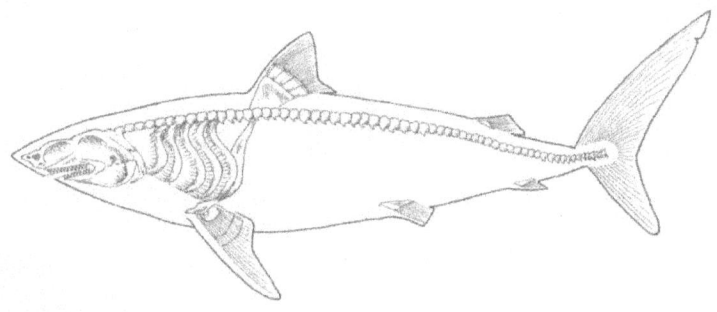

They do have a skeleton, but this too is a type of flexible tissue. The jaw, the spine, the fin—all formed from pliant stuff, the same substance as my ear or the gelatinous tip of my nose. This is not the only way the shark is assembled tenuously: the cartilaginous jaw floats freely, connected to the skull by muscle alone. It might seem like a weakness, to have a body made of something less sturdy than bone, but in this softness the shark wields their most fearsome quality: the more give in the skeleton, the wider the mouth can open.

Inside the shark mouth, anywhere from five to fifteen rows of teeth arrange themselves like an amphitheater. But with no enamel jawbone to root to like the long taps of human teeth, shark teeth sit loose in their sockets, expendable. Teeth can dislodge daily—broken on a fish skeleton or stuck in a seal belly—and a new one is immediately ready to take its place. Extra teeth from the inner rows rotate forward to fill the space of loss: a conveyor belt, the mouth a machine of new sharpness. Sharks will use and will lose more than 30,000 teeth in their lifetime. Between our two sets, most humans have 52.

Still, we have something in common, the shark and human: our teeth outlive us. After death, the cartilage of the shark body will break down swiftly, leaving only the teeth to drift away in the ever-pulling currents, a body scattered across an ocean. Then what do they become? Without the soft flex of the jaw to wield them, the teeth are no longer weapons; they are tokens, like tools kept behind glass in a museum. The tooth turns into object, a facsimile of the fear it once fed.

OBJECT (29)

We lived in a dying logging town, went roller skating every weekend. The mall was too far away, and the theater so small it fit in a barn and didn't show movies after ten. The rink was where we all went. We were twelve years old, and this was a place we could spend the whole of a Friday evening for five dollars. We straightened our hair with our mothers' irons, spreading a towel on the floor and trusting each other with hot metal near our ears. The shine was worth the occasional scalp burn, those dead cells glowing like polished teeth as we swished around the linoleum, practicing our toe-stop, our shoot-the-duck. There were always boys, of course. Jenny was dating someone older, in high school, us still sixth graders. We didn't tell our parents he'd be there with his friends, but we knew. We preened for this reason. They didn't skate, the boys—just ate nachos and occasionally glanced at us. We sat with them in a round vinyl booth, resting our strong ankles and our hips, which ached only from exercise but were becoming something else by the second, more aesthetic.

Jenny turned her head to us but kept her eyes on her boyfriend. She said, *When I brush my teeth, I never, ever gag.* Here, a threshold, to know the code of what our bodies could do. *Really?* I asked, bewildered, *I gag every time.* Jenny's boyfriend smirked, said, *That's going to be a problem one day.* The boy beside him looked me up and down, his gaze a slow roll, as tangible as if a wheel of my skate had been popped off and spun along the landscape of me, testing out the hills and give of a thing you could ride. He said, *That's a problem now.*

TOOL (25)

The tooth contains a whole world. At its core is the pulp chamber, where blood vessels and nerves intertwine, hot liquid and electricity pulsing to and fro: their own tiny tides. The nerve is where feeling happens, like the cold bite of ice cream or the tea still too hot, a spark sent from bone to brain. The pulp, then, is less citrus, more magma. Like the inner, molten heart of a planet, it is the heat that keeps the tooth alive. The pulp reaches through the end of the tooth's root and branches out into the gums, one of many anchors; the periodontal ligament, a fibrous connective tissue, binds the whole apparatus to the jawbone, which is the common denominator between teeth, tongue, muscle, skin.

Dentine makes up the bulk of the tooth, hard but still sensitive, the protective layer around the pulp. The very outer casing is the enamel: a super-strength, the body's hardest point, stronger than jaw, spine, or femur.

Holding a world together, keeping safe the softness beneath.

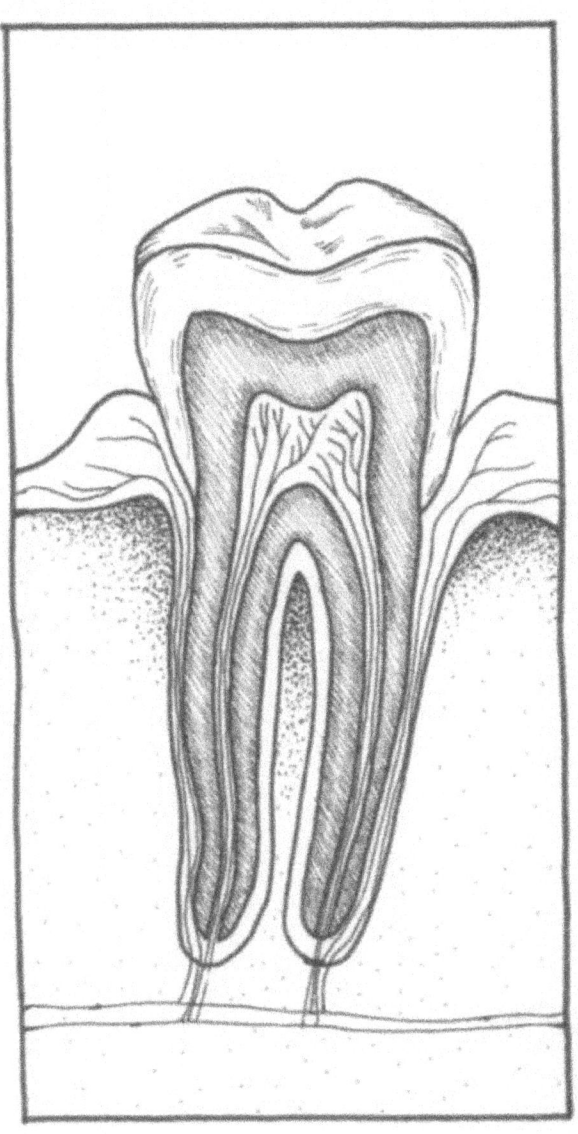

OBJECT (28)

The mouth is a site of worship. Our rural town had more churches than schools, and Sunday was as much a day of education as any. Here we learned communion; we learned what we should welcome inside of our bodies and what we should not.

Once a month, each member of the congregation would descend upon the pulpit, pew by pew, waiting our turn. We would kneel in front of the cross, choir music ringing out, awaiting the pastor's gift: a tiny plastic thimble of grape juice and a cracker thin as paper. But these were not really juice or wheat, of course. *Drink the blood of Christ*, the pastor said. *Take his flesh into your mouth.*

QUADRANT 3

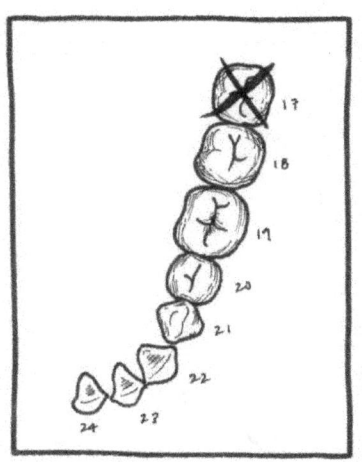

OBJECT (18)

I imagine the shark unhinging, the lower jaw untethered, lunging forward to make room for a body they are about to take apart.

I don't want to be doing this.

I want to stand up and leave, but there were so many girls vying for his attention all night; I am lucky to be the one he has on her knees. If it wasn't me, it'd be someone else. I wasn't chosen, really, just convenient, the last one he ran into after closing up the bar. When he says *less teeth,* I try to unhinge, to make room for what I don't want but know I need to be good at. Unlike the shark, what I take into my mouth I do not devour, I do not shake my great head, I do nothing with abandon.

TOOL (23)

Humans are diphyodonts, as are most mammals, meaning we only have two sets of teeth and cannot regrow them if a permanent one is lost. But elephants are an exception, regrowing their molars up to six times. Each one is the size of a brick, but it can't keep up with their diets; several sets will be eroded, this the toll of grinding down up to 300 pounds of food a day: roots, grasses, fruit, bark. When their last set becomes unusable, worn to the pulp,

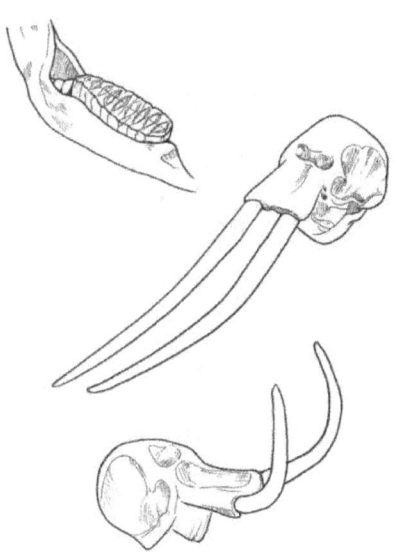

they don't survive. Tooth loss is a leading cause of death among mature elephants.

The tusks, too, are teeth—a specialized type of incisor,

made of ivory and so diffcrent in shape than the shears at the front of our mouths but coated in enamel all the same. They are used for lifting objects, fending off predators, stripping bark from trees. They continue growing throughout an elephant's lifetime, but that does not mean they are replaceable; they cannot be removed without killing the animal, needing to be carved from the skull. Yet, elephants born without tusks can survive and thrive, and the percentage of tuskless is growing—they are thought to be evolving as a response to ivory poaching. Like a message sent between generations, telling the unborn what danger awaits, to surrender what aids them before it adorns another. Not having tusks means a higher chance of survival in an environment where this tooth is killed for. For so many animals, the best defense in the face of attack is to turn your tools inward, to sever internally, to loosen parts of yourself and leave them behind.

OBJECT (19)

We had these jelly bracelets. We could buy them in packs of a hundred, every color in solid and in glitter. We would trade them, double loop them, stack them upon our arms. Before we knew what they meant, they were just an accessory, a trend. But they became endowed with meaning, given a code we had to learn, like how the wafer really meant the flesh of God. Boys would sneak attack, running down the hall or waiting for us to come out of the bathroom, hooking a finger under a bracelet and breaking it free. Whatever color they broke signaled a certain contract; no one knew who created it, we only knew that at some point, we could recite it by heart:

>yellow: hug;
>
>pink: hickey;
>
>glitter-pink: flash;
>
>orange: kiss;
>
>red: lap dance;

blue: head;

clear: anything u want.

By middle school, a girl had learned what her mouth was good for. We had seen the demonstration on a banana or cucumber. We never talked about where a mouth might go on our own bodies, never traded tips on the place a finger or a tongue might unravel us. The thought of falling to our knees for each other brought us to our knees in prayer, in fear of our wants. I knew how to swirl my tongue around the bitter rind of a fruit before I ever knew where to touch myself. The mouth is a site of worship; we were vessels, never idols.

WEAPON (22)

A shark cannot chew, only tear. Once a seal is held firm in their teeth, they shake their mighty heads. They use momentum to pull the body apart. Like a dog, in tug-of-war. The trick of centrifugal force is enough to release the flesh from bone.

It's easy to call this vicious, to see the way a seal is shredded and want to call it sick. *Predator* implies violence, implies that the shark's food sources would be better off if the shark disappeared; seal, dolphin, turtle, seagull, tuna, crustacean, mackerel, mollusk, porpoise. But when a predator population declines, the entire ecosystem suffers —prey populations boom disproportionately to their own food sources, causing widespread starvation. Thus, a seal in a shark's mouth was also dependent on the shark in life.

And not all sharks eat the same. The whale shark has the most teeth of their kind, up to three thousand at once—but these teeth are smaller and less sharp than that of carnivorous sharks: the great white, the bull, the hammerhead, the lemon. The whale shark is a filter feeder, opening wide and seeing what floats in: krill, fish eggs, shrimp, plankton. No shake of the head or cloud of blood turning the frothy ocean pink—but still we call them *Apex Predator*, defined as an animal with no *natural killers*.

What kind of killers are we? Whale sharks are an endangered species. We make language and we wield it, create collapse or distance where it suits us, conjuring absolution from a word. What if the food chain is no chain at all but a spiral or a closed loop? Tell me again about the order of things, about predation and hierarchies, about the nature of what enters between our teeth.

OBJECT (20)

We were taught that there are clear thresholds, that the seeds of womanhood are there in the body from our very beginnings, waiting to tell us what we will become. Blood, breasts, hair, hips. And what of the mouth? The same year I began to menstruate, my teeth were the strongest they had ever been.

What if I became a woman not through an event but through a slow gathering of instructions? Like splinters accumulated in the soft meat of a foot. Blood has nothing to do with it. This is about absence—a sequence of loss, then gain. Not knowing which is which.

TOOL (24)

Your milk teeth fall out not only by being pushed, as it seems, but by a set of mechanisms that break down their tether, triggered by the body's clock. The sequence of turnover begins at age five, when the gums release cells that dissolve both the ligament and the bony root that hold the baby tooth to the jaw. This breakdown is as intelligent as it is gradual—only one or two teeth are targeted at a time, leaving the rest firm until their own moment of jettison.

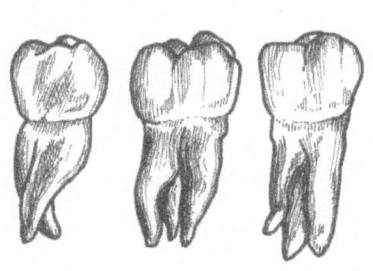

Have you ever seen an adult molar pulled free? It is alien—a calcified octopus. Yet a milk tooth fallen into a child's hand has no such tentacles; the root is disappeared in what is called *resorption*: the body eats itself, like the snake which devours their own tail. The body taking back what it formed, like its own god. When the ligament fully evaporates, only then does the milk tooth give way and come loose. You are left with a relic of your first skeleton, a softer part of yourself for keeps.

OBJECT (21)

Teeth decide what we eat. They tell us what a mouth can handle. An infant ingests only mush: applesauce, pureed carrot, smashed banana. A rotting tooth kills an appetite. Lost teeth can kill an elephant. Once, working as a server at a restaurant, I had a customer in her sixties who had just gotten braces. She ordered the chicken chowder but asked for it blended—corn, meat, green onion, and even the biscuit, all pulsed until smooth and uniform. She ate it all, not as bites but as puddles sipped from a spoon. She thanked us profusely, all the pain she was in, the limits to which her mouth had been held.

QUADRANT 2

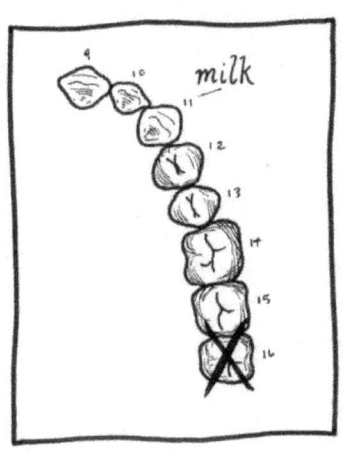

OBJECT (12)

Teeth are the most durable part of any body; they will remain when the rest of us does not. If the bartender and I stay in this position for hundreds of years, he and I in this bathroom and his hand wound in my hair, our bodies would decay—slow then quick, skin sloughing free from bone, the hand withering like fruit drying out on the ground. The collagen going softer, then gone altogether. Eventually even the skeleton would be eaten back by environment: acid, water, mineral, heat. The body breaking down to stone, to chip, to pebble, to sand: a shore made from our undoing. The hair would be released from the grip at last; it, too, would turn to soil.

The teeth, however, would stay almost exactly as they are. Shark or human; girl or predator—reduced to our most durable parts, how similar we look. Call it decoration, call it relic. Keep it beneath a pillow or wear it on a necklace.

MILK TOOTH (10)

I am also an exception among mammals: I do not have two full sets of teeth, a condition called *hypodontia,* my maxillary lateral incisors missing. I do not mean I lost them; I mean I never had them to begin with. These two adult teeth never formed, like rooms left unoccupied in the gums. Architectural issues ensued: the adult teeth I have grew in where they didn't belong, my canine seated directly next to my front tooth and ruining any chance of symmetry. At fourteen, I began a four-year endeavor of extraction, braces, surgery, and implantation that aimed to correct what had gone wrong inside me, that would make my mouth anew.

On one side, I still have a milk tooth; with no permanent tooth to signal the root to dissolve, it simply

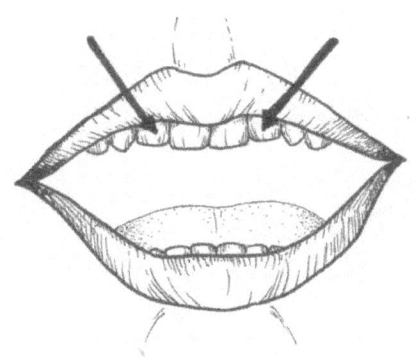

remained. Despite being a fixture in my mouth since I was ten months old, it was deemed durable, its root secure enough to last. Instead of replacing it, the dentist covered it with resin: a liquid plastic. The resin was solely to remedy the tooth's small, strange appearance—to make it look more uniform, to obscure this relic of infancy, this miracle of softness I was allowed to keep.

OBJECT (13)

It's fascinating, isn't it? The un-fixedness of mouths, how each tooth has the ability to travel, for better or worse. Like sharks rotating their teeth to the most useful locus, my gums, too, were made gelatinous. I had a perfectly healthy molar pulled. This way, there was room to move the errant canine to its correct and aesthetically pleasing location, making space to later implant a fake tooth that would mimic the incisor I was born without, to make me more even. It took months of slow migration by way of braces, the canine shifted several centimeters back, leaving a large gap.

I was sixteen and missing a tooth in the front of my mouth. It didn't help that we were rural people, no traffic light for twenty miles. Tumbleweeds bunched at every fence, an elk farm across the street from the middle school. We had dust on our boots, deerskin slung on the walls, church pews packed every Sunday, tow trucks on speed-dial for our always-dying batteries, a local rodeo the thing we were famous for. A one-horse town is primed for jokes about missing teeth. The hillbilly, the hick, the redneck. We waffled between a certain pride and shame for our town, a divide growing between who would never leave and who would never come back.

To remedy my shotgun mouth, the dentist put a fake tooth right on the wire of my braces, like a suspended fencepost. When my braces came off, the same false tooth was placed in a clear, plastic retainer that I had to wear at all times in order to keep this gap a secret. Chewing felt like using someone else's teeth, or as if my mouth was outside of my body, like a memory of eating. I ate slowly, gingerly, careful with what I bit into—the retainer being expensive to replace.

In the bathroom after meals, I would pull the plastic casing from my teeth and rinse the gunk pooled in its canyons, sometimes scrubbing this facsimile mouth with a toothbrush. If in public, I did this quickly and with my eyes down. If someone spoke to me, I would answer with my hand covering my mouth or else pretend I hadn't heard. I would cup water in my palm and bring it to my lips, rinsing and rinsing, trying to clear any substance, to make this space as empty as it had ever been.

WEAPON (11)

We are near an ocean. I can't see it, but I can hear it from where I kneel—coming in through the slatted window of the bathroom wall. A friend and I skinny dipped in that same tide the night before, salt in our mouths and the moon in our hair. After, I had walked home, nobody in my body but me.

This morning, I noticed a sign on the bulletin board by the beach entrance, warning against swimming between dusk and dawn: this is the bull sharks' time. They like to be shallow, following food closer to shore to increase the ratio of flesh to water. They are more likely to make a catch here than in the deep; they know how to manufacture a small chance of escape. The thought of those cartilaginous bodies looping between our legs, a stadium of teeth inside each mouth—maybe it was only exciting because it had already been done with no disaster. A thrill, a brush with something sharp and carnivorous, unbeknownst to us as we had waded, dipped, and splashed, looking ever more seal or octopus: all sleek curling arms and wide, meaty thighs, rolling around in the tide for the taking.

A group of sharks is called a shiver. Perhaps because of the way they move, always undulating, flicking side to side, pushing water in and out of their great, tender bodies. Or perhaps they get their name because they seek out the warm water of the shallows, yearning for a change from the cold that plumps their veins. Or maybe it's for what they do to us human animals, once safe from the reach of their throats, reading a sign that warns us not to place ourselves in the path of their feeding, a shiver moving up our spine.

RESIN (10)

I know what you're thinking—that I'm placing all these images together for you, that I'm trying to guide you toward the conclusion that this man in this bathroom was akin to a shark: a mean beast: a predator that prowled the wide expanse looking to catch prey like me. But you're wrong. I am the shark here, or I would be, if I believed in the eclipse of a metaphor. Rather, I look to the shark for answers. I wonder how we layer, the shark and I. How to be both soft and fearsome at the same time. I wonder about our teeth and about what we leave behind.

OBJECT (14)

I was not allowed a proper implant until it was believed that my jaw had stopped growing, stasis necessary to be sure that once metal was fused to bone it wouldn't shift. For almost two years, I held that negative space, waiting, hiding.

The dental surgeon deemed me ready at eighteen. Although both my parents were employed when we had begun this process four years earlier, by then they had split, had spent time out of work, and our house was set for foreclosure. Insurance called the whole thing cosmetic. And wasn't it? Or at least, it had started that way, but we were too far along, and the void they had created now needed to be filled—not only for appearance but for tension, to hold all the other teeth in their place. Without the implant to complete the scaffolding of this careful arrangement, the rest of my upper teeth would fall back into their unruly positions; a tooth has a memory, always trying to return from where it came.

The dentist burrowed into the soft meat of my mouth, like a gardener preparing to plant a new tree, one made of titanium alloy. A spiral screw was embedded into bone: one end fixed in the jaw, the other protruding from the gums. There, the crown was secured—like a cap on a mushroom stalk, or a small coronation.

My mouth became an apparatus of metal, plastic, porcelain. A masterpiece; a four-year design. What is a girl without her smile? Like a doll, my teeth felt painted on.

TOOL (9)

The temporomandibular joint acts almost as a drawbridge. It is a joint that is worked hard, the spring and pulley employed when eating, talking, yawning, brushing, flossing, grinding, smiling, sucking. Yet emotional stress burdens this point of the body as much as any mechanics. An ache germinates, a tensing at the fulcrum between the upper and lower parabolas of the mouth, causing stiffness, trying to refuse new entrance. Chronic disorders of this joint are at least twice as prevalent in people socialized as women.

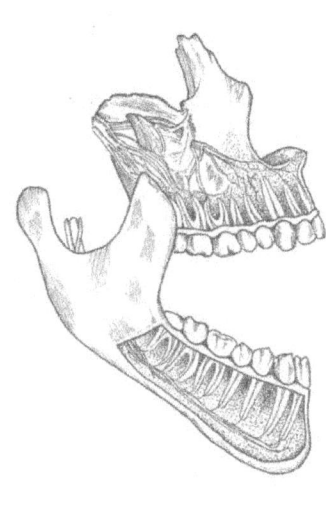

Like most bones, the jaw is not one but several: maxilla and mandible, and within each of these are more parts still. The alveolar bone is what holds the teeth, a white plane embedded with sockets. It is both plate and sponge at once: the outer layer smooth and compact; internally it is flexible and porous. The irregular hollows resemble limestone by the sea, rock weathered like honeycomb from salt spray.

Here, negative space allows the bone more give; to absorb the hardest impact, emptiness is key.

OBJECT (15)

The more we tried to make my mouth pretty, the less useful my mouth became. I had once been able to cleave a fault line in the globe of an apple, slice meat from where it clung to a thigh; once I could no longer access their utility, I knew the role of each tooth more intimately. The canines are the weapons, like knifepoints, they puncture and tear; the incisors, chisel-shaped, cut and shear; the molars mash, like mortar and pestle, grinding down food in preparation for the throat's long tunnel. Each tooth a ritual.

For some, hypodontia affects function—the ability to eat and which foods. For me, this wasn't the case. My teeth had functioned perfectly *before*. The reason to shift the geography of my mouth was to correct what looked wrong. But don't be fooled: that does not mean it wasn't essential. The dentist, the oral surgeon, my parents, myself—we knew that survival isn't just about what you can sink your teeth into. Sometimes you are the apple to be bitten, the flesh that will make mouths water—being

appealing as important as any of the body's tools.

QUADRANT 1

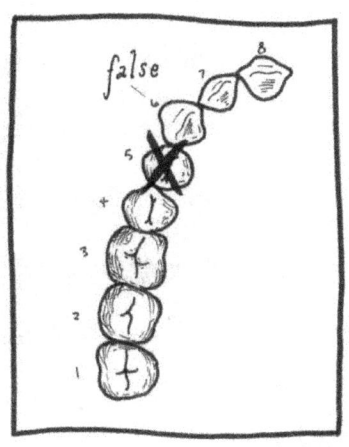

OBJECT (4)

I continue to kneel quietly. My teeth not tools but nuisance.

How I had longed for a full mouth for so many years and now he can't get off, my bones in the way. He sighs. He leaves me here, the small canyons between the tiles now embedded in my knees, another displacement of my body to make space for something else. This is not the first time, and it won't be the last. He could be anyone. I wipe my mouth. I run my thumb along the edge of my maxillary incisors. Feel their sharpness and can't discern between the true and the false.

FALSE TOOTH (7)

Predator:

1. an animal that naturally preys on others
2. a person or group that ruthlessly exploits others

The word *predator* is slippery, a wet thing, oozing like an oil spill—the same noun used for animals who eat for survival and for a man who puts a woman on her knees, who knows well that he need only press lightly on her shoulder.

By this logic, the shark exploits the seal; the wolf, the deer; the bear, the salmon. Ruthless and coercive. Or: the bartender with his hand on my neck is only doing what is natural to his kind. Is the shark or the man the metaphor? An eclipse of meaning, of the ways bodies are shred. Words are no accidents: see the little skulls we construct, see their fake teeth in full sets.

OBJECT (3)

Before I had the permanent tooth placed, the titanium screw was first affixed with a temporary crown, to train the gums how to mold around it. Another interval, another impermanence to be precious with. The temporary was weakly attached, easily ripped out on an errant bite. Corn on the cob, the apple on its core, raw carrots, beef jerky, thick-crusted breads—if its flesh needed to be torn from a firm hold, I could not eat it. Only small bites that could be ground by the molars, everything pushed back toward the throat. The canines with nothing to knife, the incisors with nothing to shear, for years. I employed my mouth gingerly, every entrance calculated. At sixteen, I was no stranger to dieting; it was easy to justify restriction when what I could eat was already so limited. I bought expensive packets of powdered meals that magically turned into soups, smoothies, pancakes. Soft things with a deficit in calories. Disappear, disappear.

WEAPON (6)

In Florida, a lemon shark was observed with a fish stringer—a hooked spear connected to a steel wire—impaled near their pectoral fin. The shark must have caught on the contraption then easily snapped the wire, one good tug with muscle made strong by constant oscillation. But the spear stuck, embedded in the meat of the shark's gut. Scientists watched the lemon shark for 435 days; over this period the steel was slowly, miraculously, expelled, pushed free simply by the slow workings of the cartilaginous body. Softness, once again, made survival.

Afterward, the only evidence of injury was a long scar in the shark's skin, skin which appears slick as water but is actually like sandpaper to the touch, made up of structures called *dermal denticles*. The root of this word is intentional—denticles are scales that make an extremely durable armor, shaped as they are like grooved teeth. Like an extra mouth making up the entire perimeter of the shark's body, the skin-teeth spat out that metal splinter.

A foreign object is embedded in my body: every day, my cells must agree with this tooth that doesn't belong to me. Every day is another chance at rejection, of the mouth crying *alert* and pushing the metal through tissue. It's uncommon but it happens. Once, in the span of a single afternoon, my earlobe pushed the metal hook of my jewelry almost clear through the flesh, creating its own track: the hole in which I hung the earring now a long dash, my body finding a way to dispel this foreign material. The skin its own agent, rejecting unwanted entrance.

OBJECT (2)

The mouth holds survival like a sore, or a loose tooth: the tongue unable to resist further disturbance, worrying it over and over to see if anything has changed. Tenderness a reminder of what is at stake.

>Breathe,
>
>eat,
>
>drink,
>
>bite,
>
>cleave,
>
>speak,
>
>smile,
>
>suck.

TOOL (8)

The canine is the sharpest of our teeth, its pointed tip something we have in common with almost all the animals called *Apex Predator*. The wolf is an obvious example, this tooth being named for the canid after all. But the shape of the canine tooth is found across most of the vertebrates in the animal kingdom—the mammal, reptile, fish, and amphibian classes each have creatures who cause fear with their pointed mouths.

Yet this our sharpest tool is the last to grow in among humans; incisors and molars all emerge first, leaving a gap where the canine should be until we're a year and a half old. When the permanent teeth break skin, the canines are last to arrive again. These thresholds decide what can enter our bodies—a time between milk and meat, between soft and slice. For other mammals called predator, this is also when they are left most vulnerable—sharp teeth an apparatus for attack and defense. For humans, the variation between canine and incisor is less important—some even choose to shave these points down, to opt for uniformity. For us, these thresholds mark the last moments when our teeth will be considered for their utility alone. For whom is my mouth still a tool? I am permeable. I am decided upon. My teeth jewels to be worn.

OBJECT (1)

It is still night. I walk to the edge of the ocean, the cusp of the bull sharks' feeding ground. I wade in, feel their coolness leach warmth from the water, my ankles growing chilled. I don't remove all my clothes but rather I strip back my skin, my lip, my cheekbone. The body rendered down. So many jaws at my feet, circling. These tools we have, see how they wield them. How I long to flip my body over and see each scale, each regenerated cell, my animal. To shift my usefulness back inside myself. No relic or necklace. To know my own mechanisms: knife, chisel, shear. I show my teeth. I cause a shiver.

Acknowledgments

Thank you, firstly and wholly, to Professor Lily Hoang—for reading a brief essay I wrote about milk teeth and encouraging me to tunnel deeper into this strange site of examination; for helping me weather the emotional, institutional, and physical fatigue of graduate school during a pandemic; for making me believe in my own vision. You are the fiercest educator I've ever had, and your generosity is the model by which I operate my own classroom.

Thank you to Emily Yang for reading my first draft during a graduate workshop held on Zoom, before we'd ever even met, and reminding me that this piece is as much about the soft parts we must keep as it is about the titanium ones we've had to adopt.

Thank you to Adriana Tosun for always reading my work with such attention, for talking me through structural experiments, for our shared inclination toward the strange and unruly. My colleague, my friend, my collaborator. I'm so grateful for you.

Thank you to T Bambrick, my longtime friend and poet idol, for once saying the phrase, "eclipse of a metaphor," to me during a conversation about queerness, visibility, and language. That phrase has forever changed the way I think of words, from a map to a full political landscape, sky and all.

Thank you to Beth Carlson for creating the custom artwork in these pages—what a joy to have such talent and generosity in a dear friend. Thank you for making this work ours.

And thank you to *Small Harbor Publishing* for seeing something worthwhile here and reviving this little chapbook at what I thought was its end. If not for you, Allison and Josh, this work would have been long abandoned. Thank you.

Becca Rae Rose is a triple fire sign, cribbage player, and a wannabe wildlife biologist. She's a graduate of the MFA Program in Writing at UC San Diego and a co-founder of (*peel lit*) and *KALEIDOSCOPED MAG*. Her work has appeared in *Western Humanities Review*, *Swamp Ape Review*, and *PANK*. She lives and teaches in San Diego, where she's working on a novel about bats.

About Small Harbor Publishing

Small Harbor Publishing is a 501c3 nonprofit organization. Our goal is to publish unique and diverse voices. We are a feminist press, and we are committed to diversity and inclusion. We strive to bring new voices to a devoted and expanding readership.

Small Harbor Publishing began in 2018 with the first issue of *Harbor Review*. The magazine is an online space where poetry and art converse. *Harbor Review* quickly grew and now publishes reviews and runs multiple micro chapbook competitions, including the Washburn Prize and the Editor's Prize.

In July 2020, Small Harbor Publishing was officially incorporated and began Harbor Editions. Harbor Editions accepts submissions through a chapbook open reading period, a hybrid chapbook open reading period, the Marginalia Series, and the Laureate Prize.

In 2023, Harbor Anthologies began with a mission to promote texts that explore social justice issues and highlight marginalized writers.

If you would like to support Small Harbor Publishing, visit our "About" page at: smallharborpublishing.com/about.

www.ingramcontent.com/pod-product-compliance
Lightning Source LLC
Chambersburg PA
CBHW051702040426
42446CB00009B/1267